Split of Mind

R.R Esther

Presentation by *BookLeaf Publishing*

Web: www.bookleafpub.com

E-mail: info@bookleafpub.com

ISBN: 9789395969017

First edition 2022

this is dedicated to inspiration and my love,
j.m.

ACKNOWLEDGEMENT

I'd like to acknowledge the plenty of inspirations and the people that have impacted me to write this book. My father who has mentored me where I now can appreciate the sense of life and to have no worry of death. My mother who has taught me to be comforting and to love as much as I can. My best friend, D.R., who's still in my life that shaped my childhood and still regains more memories onto life. Finally, J.M., my partner in life and whom I choose to go through time with. The kindest blue eyes as fierce as the ocean tide, and the love of my life. Thank you for impacting my life and inspire me to write my story.

PREFACE

As you read throughout the collection of poems, I want you to have this reminder: these experiences do not define me, and should they never define you. Traumatic events can often deceive us into thinking that experience was in our control. However, though, it was never in our control and we cannot let that interfere with the control we have now. The purpose of these poems, these strings of rhyme, is to give comfort and closure that someone else has gotten stronger. Through time you'll find that you don't need to exist, you can live.

stay alive.

White Serpent

A white serpent collides into the Persian Moon
It's pain is so soft and true
She bathed herself under it's streams of light
And released herself into the silhouettes of the
night.

A face so fearful now interwoven in wool
Her eyes finally softened into the color of a
paled jewel
A blackening morning roared a dolorous bell
A white serpent knew her too well.

R.R Esther

thieves guild

theft of my body
and bleak of my soul
you took everything just so you can feel
you took what you can steal

my innocence.

R.R Esther.

silence

3

not yet i could've heard the echoing of regret
that would have become that day
not yet i could've heard the reverberating silence
that i wish would be okay.

R.R Esther

life

4

if life were so beautiful
why do some cut flowers?

R.R Esther

martensitic steel

5

defenseless as my wrists
i look at the blue hue of my skin
  i still feel the familiar sting
 of what it means to win
of what it means to control
 of it what it means to feel.

R.R Esther

a winters tulip

longing for what it would be as a tulip in winter
crippling of my peddles frosting my vein
bits fall onto the ground
and in no way would i be admired
but picked up
then thrown away

then,
i think,
i have always been this way.

R.R Esther

freedom

trees wresting with the wind in a fright
with a blue haze in the middle of hills
silhouettes restlessly move into the night
colors combust into rain, in my dream that i see
before the dawn breaks, how i wonder
how freedom could be?

R.R Esther

stain

8

you stained my skin
with your touch
i felt your anger and insecurity with your hand
my innocence fell into your hands
and forever stained apart of my soul.

R.R Esther

Thousand Corpses

A thousand corpses were conjured in a gallery
The sculptor raises his clay to make them appear
Some faces are long, intense, and confused
Some faces are soft, kind, and in fear

They speak to each other one by one:
"Why is that I hang in this hall?,"
"How am I living without feeling at all?,"
"Can you see and hear me?,"
"Why can't you hear and see me?,"

The sculpture makes his silver and gold
And puts away all his creations into a furnace
To have their man-made flesh melt into a mold
And he leaves for the day
And leaves all the thousand corpses away.

R.R Esther

All Of It Is Pesticide

A creature with a smooth harden shell leaks
Soaking my blood vessels into their own flesh
They hatch every second, every minute, every
half of the last minute
Peeling away into my sight
Moving frighteningly, scattering on my bedroom
floor
All of them experiencing a new life born, and a
new death that scorns

A burial ground underneath my finger nails lay
They couldn't experience the life they've been
promised
From the flies protecting their young
From the widows defending their own flesh
From all the pests
A little pill flicks them to knowing death

All of it is
pesticide

R.R Esther

"Love,"

Love is the answer.
Love.

R.R Esther

silence

at 4:35 am, right before everyone's lives begin
stillness as your eyes can see
and silence before the day begins
that's the beauty of life
stillness
silence.

R.R Esther

lunar

if the moon can glow while the sun shines
you can be what they are
glowing still in the ray of darkness
and shining as the day has begun.

R.R Esther

regret

i want anyone to know
you are still just as magnificent
when they are still regretting what they did to
you.

R.R Esther

determine

think of future like this:
you see dust moving down a hallway
and it's moving rapidly
only the laws of physics and wind could ever
determine what will happen
neither you or the dust can decide.

forget about tomorrow and dream for today.

R.R Esther.

revolution

16

you can emancipate yourself from war
you can free yourself from chaos
if you want it.

R.R Esther

grocery store

i walk into the store with you
and you Immediately run towards the flowers
the glimmering store lights shine on the peddles
the yellow sunflowers moving into red roses
your blue eyes grow larger to the details
how could i ever forget you?

R.R Esther

j.m.

18

Your eyes swallows all of the dulling light
It's dreaming, it's flowing, and fearless
The way you sing bleeds into the night
It's soft, it's joyful, and endearing
Your mind blows up a thousand of clovers
It's obscure, wild, and beautiful

R.R Esther

d.r.

we walked into the building together as strangers
feeling nervous and afraid
feeling hurt and confused as the years went by
but you changed my life
you never made me feel any different
you never acted embarrassed to be around me
then we left together
as best friends, 7 years later.

thank you.

R.R Esther

when the tiger broke free

after all of these years of torment and mental
tissue
i found what i've always been looking for.
what it means to be free.
and it isn't the soldiers breaching
and it isn't the outlaw riding into the sun

i woke up one day and started to smile.
"i'm okay."
"i'm happy."
"i'm fine."

i longed for this day.
i am free.

R.R Esther.